A Blot In The 'Scutcheon' by Robert Browning

A Tragedy

Bells and Pomegranates Number V

Robert Browning is one of the most significant Victorian Poets and, of course, English Poetry.

Much of his reputation is based upon his mastery of the dramatic monologue although his talents encompassed verse plays and even a well-regarded essay on Shelley during a long and prolific career.

He was born on May 7th, 1812 in Walmouth, London. Much of his education was home based and Browning was an eclectic and studious student, learning several languages and much else across a myriad of subjects, interests and passions.

Browning's early career began promisingly. The fragment from his intended long poem Pauline brought him to the attention of Dante Gabriel Rossetti, and was followed by Paracelsus, which was praised by both William Wordsworth and Charles Dickens. In 1840 the difficult Sordello, which was seen as willfully obscure, brought his career almost to a standstill.

Despite these artistic and professional difficulties his personal life was about to become immensely fulfilling. He began a relationship with, and then married, the older and better known Elizabeth Barrett. This new foundation served to energise his writings, his life and his career.

During their time in Italy they both wrote much of their best work. With her untimely death in 1861 he returned to London and thereafter began several further major projects.

The collection Dramatis Personae (1864) and the book-length epic poem The Ring and the Book (1868-69) were published and well received; his reputation as a venerated English poet now assured.

Robert Browning died in Venice on December 12th, 1889.

Index of Contents

MILDRED TRESHAM.
GUENDOLEN TRESHAM.
THOROLD, Earl Tresham.
AUSTIN TRESHAM.
HENRY, Earl Mertoun.
GERARD, and other retainers of Lord Tresham.

ACT I

SCENE I.—The Interior of a Lodge in Lord Tresham's Park

Many Retainers crowded at the window, supposed to command a view of the entrance to his Mansion.

GERARD, the Warrener, his back to a table on which are flagons, etc.

FIRST RETAINER
Ay, do! push, friends, and then you'll push down me!
—What for? Does any hear a runner's foot
Or a steed's trample or a coach-wheel's cry?
Is the Earl come or his least poursuivant?
But there's no breeding in a man of you
Save Gerard yonder: here's a half-place yet,
Old Gerard!

GERARD
Save your courtesies, my friend. Here is my place.

SECOND RETAINER
Now, Gerard, out with it!
What makes you sullen, this of all the days
I' the year? To-day that young rich bountiful
Handsome Earl Mertoun, whom alone they match
With our Lord Tresham through the country-side,
Is coming here in utmost bravery
To ask our master's sister's hand?

GERARD
What then?

SECOND RETAINER
What then? Why, you, she speaks to, if she meets
Your worship, smiles on as you hold apart

The boughs to let her through her forest walks,
You, always favourite for your no-deserts,
You've heard, these three days, how Earl Mertoun sues
To lay his heart and house and broad lands too
At Lady Mildred's feet: and while we squeeze
Ourselves into a mousehole lest we miss
One congee of the least page in his train,
You sit o' one side—"there's the Earl," say I—
"What then?" say you!

THIRD RETAINER
I'll wager he has let
Both swans he tamed for Lady Mildred swim
Over the falls and gain the river!

GERARD
Ralph,
Is not to-morrow my inspecting-day
For you and for your hawks?

FOURTH RETAINER
Let Gerard be!
He's coarse-grained, like his carved black cross-bow stock.
Ha, look now, while we squabble with him, look!
Well done, now—is not this beginning, now,
To purpose?

FIRST RETAINER
Our retainers look as fine—
That's comfort. Lord, how Richard holds himself
With his white staff! Will not a knave behind
Prick him upright?

FOURTH RETAINER
He's only bowing, fool!
The Earl's man bent us lower by this much.

FIRST RETAINER
That's comfort. Here's a very cavalcade!

THIRD RETAINER
I don't see wherefore Richard, and his troop
Of silk and silver varlets there, should find
Their perfumed selves so indispensable
On high days, holidays! Would it so disgrace
Our family, if I, for instance, stood—
In my right hand a cast of Swedish hawks,
A leash of greyhounds in my left?—

GERARD
With Hugh
The logman for supporter, in his right
The bill-hook, in his left the brushwood-shears!

THIRD RETAINER
Out on you, crab! What next, what next? The Earl!

FIRST RETAINER
Oh Walter, groom, our horses, do they match
The Earl's? Alas, that first pair of the six—
They paw the ground—Ah Walter! and that brute
Just on his haunches by the wheel!

SIXTH RETAINER
Ay—ay!
You, Philip, are a special hand, I hear,
At soups and sauces: what's a horse to you?
D'ye mark that beast they've slid into the midst
So cunningly?—then, Philip, mark this further;
No leg has he to stand on!

FIRST RETAINER
No? that's comfort.

SECOND RETAINER
Peace, Cook! The Earl descends. Well, Gerard, see
The Earl at least! Come, there's a proper man,
I hope! Why, Ralph, no falcon, Pole or Swede,
Has got a starrier eye.

THIRD RETAINER
His eyes are blue:
But leave my hawks alone!

FOURTH RETAINER
So young, and yet
So tall and shapely!

FIFTH RETAINER
Here's Lord Tresham's self!
There now—there's what a nobleman should be!
He's older, graver, loftier, he's more like
A House's head.

SECOND RETAINER
But you'd not have a boy

—And what's the Earl beside?—possess too soon
That stateliness?

FIRST RETAINER
Our master takes his hand—
Richard and his white staff are on the move—
Back fall our people—(tsh!—there's Timothy
Sure to get tangled in his ribbon-ties,
And Peter's cursed rosette's a-coming off!)
—At last I see our lord's back and his friend's;
And the whole beautiful bright company
Close round them—in they go!

[Jumping down from the window-bench, and making for the table and its jugs.

Good health, long life,
Great joy to our Lord Tresham and his House!

SIXTH RETAINER
My father drove his father first to court,
After his marriage-day—ay, did he!

SECOND RETAINER
God bless
Lord Tresham, Lady Mildred, and the Earl!
Here, Gerard, reach your beaker!

GERARD
Drink, my boys!
Don't mind me—all's not right about me—drink!

SECOND RETAINER [aside]
He's vexed, now, that he let the show escape!
[To **GERARD**]
Remember that the Earl returns this way.

GERARD
That way?

SECOND RETAINER
Just so.

GERARD
Then my way's here.

[Goes.

SECOND RETAINER

Old Gerard
Will die soon—mind, I said it! He was used
To care about the pitifullest thing
That touched the House's honour, not an eye
But his could see wherein: and on a cause
Of scarce a quarter this importance, Gerard
Fairly had fretted flesh and bone away
In cares that this was right, nor that was wrong,
Such point decorous, and such square by rule—
He knew such niceties, no herald more:
And now—you see his humour: die he will!

SECOND RETAINER
God help him! Who's for the great servants' hall
To hear what's going on inside! They'd follow
Lord Tresham into the saloon.

THIRD RETAINER
I!—

FOURTH RETAINER
I!—
Leave Frank alone for catching, at the door,
Some hint of how the parley goes inside!
Prosperity to the great House once more!
Here's the last drop!

FIRST RETAINER
Have at you! Boys, hurrah!

SCENE II.—A Saloon in the Mansion

Enter **LORD TRESHAM**, **LORD MERTOUN**, **AUSTIN**, and **GUENDOLEN**

TRESHAM
I welcome you, Lord Mertoun, yet once more,
To this ancestral roof of mine. Your name
—Noble among the noblest in itself,
Yet taking in your person, fame avers,
New price and lustre,—(as that gem you wear,
Transmitted from a hundred knightly breasts,
Fresh chased and set and fixed by its last lord,
Seems to re-kindle at the core)—your name
Would win you welcome!—

MERTOUN

Thanks!

TRESHAM
But add to that,
The worthiness and grace and dignity
Of your proposal for uniting both
Our Houses even closer than respect
Unites them now—add these, and you must grant
One favour more, nor that the least,—to think
The welcome I should give;—'tis given! My lord,
My only brother, Austin: he's the king's.
Our cousin, Lady Guendolen—betrothed
To Austin: all are yours.

MERTOUN
I thank you—less
For the expressed commendings which your seal,
And only that, authenticates—forbids
My putting from me... to my heart I take
Your praise... but praise less claims my gratitude,
Than the indulgent insight it implies
Of what must needs be uppermost with one
Who comes, like me, with the bare leave to ask,
In weighed and measured unimpassioned words,
A gift, which, if as calmly 'tis denied,
He must withdraw, content upon his cheek,
Despair within his soul. That I dare ask
Firmly, near boldly, near with confidence
That gift, I have to thank you. Yes, Lord Tresham,
I love your sister—as you'd have one love
That lady... oh more, more I love her! Wealth,
Rank, all the world thinks me, they're yours, you know,
To hold or part with, at your choice—but grant
My true self, me without a rood of land,
A piece of gold, a name of yesterday,
Grant me that lady, and you... Death or life?

GUENDOLEN [apart to **AUSTIN**]
Why, this is loving,
Austin!

AUSTIN
He's so young!

GUENDOLEN
Young? Old enough, I think, to half surmise
He never had obtained an entrance here,
Were all this fear and trembling needed.

AUSTIN
Hush!
He reddens.

GUENDOLEN
Mark him, Austin; that's true love!
Ours must begin again.

TRESHAM
We'll sit, my lord.
Ever with best desert goes diffidence.
I may speak plainly nor be misconceived
That I am wholly satisfied with you
On this occasion, when a falcon's eye
Were dull compared with mine to search out faults,
Is somewhat. Mildred's hand is hers to give
Or to refuse.

MERTOUN
But you, you grant my suit?
I have your word if hers?

TRESHAM
My best of words
If hers encourage you. I trust it will.
Have you seen Lady Mildred, by the way?

MERTOUN
I... I... our two demesnes, remember, touch,
I have beer used to wander carelessly
After my stricken game: the heron roused
Deep in my woods, has trailed its broken wing
Thro' thicks and glades a mile in yours,—or else
Some eyass ill-reclaimed has taken flight
And lured me after her from tree to tree,
I marked not whither. I have come upon
The lady's wondrous beauty unaware,
And—and then... I have seen her.

GUENDOLEN [aside to **AUSTIN**]
Note that mode
Of faltering out that, when a lady passed,
He, having eyes, did see her! You had said—
"On such a day I scanned her, head to foot;
Observed a red, where red should not have been,
Outside her elbow; but was pleased enough
Upon the whole." Let such irreverent talk

Be lessoned for the future!

TRESHAM
What's to say
May be said briefly. She has never known
A mother's care; I stand for father too.
Her beauty is not strange to you, it seems—
You cannot know the good and tender heart,
Its girl's trust and its woman's constancy,
How pure yet passionate, how calm yet kind,
How grave yet joyous, how reserved yet free
As light where friends are—how imbued with lore
The world most prizes, yet the simplest, yet
The... one might know I talked of Mildred—thus
We brothers talk!

MERTOUN
I thank you.

TRESHAM
In a word,
Control's not for this lady; but her wish
To please me outstrips in its subtlety
My power of being pleased: herself creates
The want she means to satisfy. My heart
Prefers your suit to her as 'twere its own.
Can I say more?

MERTOUN
No more—thanks, thanks—no more!

TRESHAM
This matter then discussed...

MERTOUN
We'll waste no breath
On aught less precious. I'm beneath the roof
Which holds her: while I thought of that, my speech
To you would wander—as it must not do,
Since as you favour me I stand or fall.
I pray you suffer that I take my leave!

TRESHAM
With less regret 'tis suffered, that again
We meet, I hope, so shortly.

MERTOUN
We? again?—

Ah yes, forgive me—when shall... you will crown
Your goodness by forthwith apprising me
When... if... the lady will appoint a day
For me to wait on you—and her.

TRESHAM
So soon
As I am made acquainted with her thoughts
On your proposal—howsoe'er they lean—
A messenger shall bring you the result.

MERTOUN
You cannot bind me more to you, my lord.
Farewell till we renew... I trust, renew
A converse ne'er to disunite again.

TRESHAM
So may it prove!

MERTOUN
You, lady, you, sir, take
My humble salutation!

GUENDOLEN and **AUSTIN**
Thanks!

TRESHAM
Within there!

[**SERVANTS** enter. **TRESHAM** conducts **MERTOUN** to the door.

[Meantime **AUSTIN** remarks

—Well,
Here I have an advantage of the Earl,
Confess now! I'd not think that all was safe
Because my lady's brother stood my friend!
Why, he makes sure of her—"do you say yes—
She'll not say, no,"—what comes it to beside?
I should have prayed the brother, "speak this speech,
For Heaven's sake urge this on her—put in this—
Forget not, as you'd save me, t'other thing,—
Then set down what she says, and how she looks,
And if she smiles, and" (in an under breath)
"Only let her accept me, and do you
And all the world refuse me, if you dare!"

GUENDOLEN

That way you'd take, friend Austin? What a shame
I was your cousin, tamely from the first
Your bride, and all this fervour's run to waste!
Do you know you speak sensibly to-day?
The Earl's a fool.

AUSTIN
Here's Thorold. Tell him so!

TRESHAM [returning]
Now, voices, voices! 'St! the lady's first!
How seems he?—seems he not... come, faith give fraud
The mercy-stroke whenever they engage!
Down with fraud, up with faith! How seems the Earl?
A name! a blazon! if you knew their worth,
As you will never! come—the Earl?

GUENDOLEN
He's young.

TRESHAM
What's she? an infant save in heart and brain.
Young! Mildred is fourteen, remark! And you...
Austin, how old is she?

GUENDOLEN
There's tact for you!
I meant that being young was good excuse
If one should tax him...

TRESHAM
Well?

GUENDOLEN
With lacking wit.

TRESHAM
He lacked wit? Where might he lack wit, so please you?

GUENDOLEN
In standing straighter than the steward's rod
And making you the tiresomest harangue,
Instead of slipping over to my side
And softly whispering in my ear, "Sweet lady,
Your cousin there will do me detriment
He little dreams of: he's absorbed, I see,
In my old name and fame—be sure he'll leave
My Mildred, when his best account of me

Is ended, in full confidence I wear
My grandsire's periwig down either cheek.
I'm lost unless your gentleness vouchsafes"...

TRESHAM

..."To give a best of best accounts, yourself,
Of me and my demerits." You are right!
He should have said what now I say for him.
Yon golden creature, will you help us all?
Here's Austin means to vouch for much, but you
—You are... what Austin only knows! Come up,
All three of us: she's in the library
No doubt, for the day's wearing fast. Precede!

GUENDOLEN

Austin, how we must—!

TRESHAM

Must what? Must speak truth,
Malignant tongue! Detect one fault in him!
I challenge you!

GUENDOLEN

Witchcraft's a fault in him,
For you're bewitched.

TRESHAM

What's urgent we obtain
Is, that she soon receive him—say, to-morrow—,
Next day at furthest.

GUENDOLEN

Ne'er instruct me!

TRESHAM

Come!
—He's out of your good graces, since forsooth,
He stood not as he'd carry us by storm
With his perfections! You're for the composed
Manly assured becoming confidence!
—Get her to say, "to-morrow," and I'll give you...
I'll give you black Urganda, to be spoiled
With petting and snail-paces. Will you? Come!

SCENE III.—Mildred's Chamber. A Painted Window Overlooks the Park

MILDRED and **GUENDOLEN**

GUENDOLEN
Now, Mildred, spare those pains. I have not left
Our talkers in the library, and climbed
The wearisome ascent to this your bower
In company with you,—I have not dared...
Nay, worked such prodigies as sparing you
Lord Mertoun's pedigree before the flood,
Which Thorold seemed in very act to tell
—Or bringing Austin to pluck up that most
Firm-rooted heresy—your suitor's eyes,
He would maintain, were grey instead of blue—
I think I brought him to contrition!—Well,
I have not done such things, (all to deserve
A minute's quiet cousin's talk with you,)
To be dismissed so coolly.

MILDRED
Guendolen!
What have I done? what could suggest...

GUENDOLEN
There, there!
Do I not comprehend you'd be alone
To throw those testimonies in a heap,
Thorold's enlargings, Austin's brevities,
With that poor silly heartless Guendolen's
Ill-time misplaced attempted smartnesses—
And sift their sense out? now, I come to spare you
Nearly a whole night's labour. Ask and have!
Demand, be answered! Lack I ears and eyes?
Am I perplexed which side of the rock-table
The Conqueror dined on when he landed first,
Lord Mertoun's ancestor was bidden take—
The bow-hand or the arrow-hand's great meed?
Mildred, the Earl has soft blue eyes!

MILDRED
My brother—
Did he... you said that he received him well?

GUENDOLEN
If I said only "well" I said not much.
Oh, stay—which brother?

MILDRED
Thorold! who—Who else?

GUENDOLEN

Thorold (a secret) is too proud by half,—
Nay, hear me out—with us he's even gentler
Than we are with our birds. Of this great House
The least retainer that e'er caught his glance
Would die for him, real dying—no mere talk:
And in the world, the court, if men would cite
The perfect spirit of honour, Thorold's name
Rises of its clear nature to their lips.
But he should take men's homage, trust in it,
And care no more about what drew it down.
He has desert, and that, acknowledgment;
Is he content?

MILDRED

You wrong him, Guendolen.

GUENDOLEN

He's proud, confess; so proud with brooding o'er
The light of his interminable line,
An ancestry with men all paladins,
And women all...

MILDRED

Dear Guendolen, 'tis late!
When yonder purple pane the climbing moon
Pierces, I know 'tis midnight.

GUENDOLEN

Well, that Thorold
Should rise up from such musings, and receive
One come audaciously to graft himself
Into this peerless stock, yet find no flaw,
No slightest spot in such an one...

MILDRED

Who finds
A spot in Mertoun?

GUENDOLEN

Not your brother; therefore,
Not the whole world.

MILDRED

I am weary, Guendolen.
Bear with me!

GUENDOLEN
I am foolish.

MILDRED
Oh no, kind!
But I would rest.

GUENDOLEN
Good night and rest to you!
I said how gracefully his mantle lay
Beneath the rings of his light hair?

MILDRED
Brown hair.

GUENDOLEN
Brown? why, it IS brown: how could you know that?

MILDRED
How? did not you—Oh, Austin 'twas, declared
His hair was light, not brown—my head!—and look,
The moon-beam purpling the dark chamber! Sweet,
Good night!

GUENDOLEN
Forgive me—sleep the soundlier for me!

[Going, she turns suddenly.

Mildred!
Perdition! all's discovered! Thorold finds
—That the Earl's greatest of all grandmothers
Was grander daughter still—to that fair dame
Whose garter slipped down at the famous dance!

[Goes.

MILDRED
Is she—can she be really gone at last?
My heart! I shall not reach the window. Needs
Must I have sinned much, so to suffer.

[She lifts the small lamp which is suspended before the Virgin's image in the window, and places it by the purple pane.

There!

[She returns to the seat in front.

Mildred and Mertoun! Mildred, with consent
Of all the world and Thorold, Mertoun's bride!
Too late! 'Tis sweet to think of, sweeter still
To hope for, that this blessed end soothes up
The curse of the beginning; but I know
It comes too late: 'twill sweetest be of all
To dream my soul away and die upon.

[A noise without.

The voice! Oh why, why glided sin the snake
Into the paradise Heaven meant us both?

[The window opens softly. A low voice sings.

There's a woman like a dew-drop, she's so purer than the purest;
And her noble heart's the noblest, yes, and her sure faith's the surest:
And her eyes are dark and humid, like the depth on depth of lustre
Hid i' the harebell, while her tresses, sunnier than the wild-grape cluster,
Gush in golden tinted plenty down her neck's rose-misted marble:
Then her voice's music... call it the well's bubbling, the bird's warble!

[A FIGURE wrapped in a mantle appears at the window.

And this woman says, "My days were sunless and my nights were moonless,
Parched the pleasant April herbage, and the lark's heart's outbreak tuneless,
If you loved me not!" And I who—(ah, for words of flame!) adore her,
Who am mad to lay my spirit prostrate palpably before her—

[He enters, approaches her seat, and bends over her.

I may enter at her portal soon, as now her lattice takes me,
And by noontide as by midnight make her mine, as hers she makes me!

[The EARL throws off his slouched hat and long cloak.

My very heart sings, so I sing, Beloved!

MILDRED
Sit, Henry—do not take my hand!

MERTOUN
'Tis mine.
The meeting that appalled us both so much
Is ended.

MILDRED

What begins now?

MERTOUN
Happiness
Such as the world contains not.

MILDRED
That is it.
Our happiness would, as you say, exceed
The whole world's best of blisses: we—do we
Deserve that? Utter to your soul, what mine
Long since, Beloved, has grown used to hear,
Like a death-knell, so much regarded once,
And so familiar now; this will not be!

MERTOUN
Oh, Mildred, have I met your brother's face?
Compelled myself—if not to speak untruth,
Yet to disguise, to shun, to put aside
The truth, as—what had e'er prevailed on me
Save you to venture? Have I gained at last
Your brother, the one scarer of your dreams,
And waking thoughts' sole apprehension too?
Does a new life, like a young sunrise, break
On the strange unrest of our night, confused
With rain and stormy flaw—and will you see
No dripping blossoms, no fire-tinted drops
On each live spray, no vapour steaming up,
And no expressless glory in the East?
When I am by you, to be ever by you,
When I have won you and may worship you,
Oh, Mildred, can you say "this will not be"?

MILDRED
Sin has surprised us, so will punishment.

MERTOUN
No—me alone, who sinned alone!

MILDRED
The night
You likened our past life to—was it storm
Throughout to you then, Henry?

MERTOUN
Of your life
I spoke—what am I, what my life, to waste
A thought about when you are by me?—you

It was, I said my folly called the storm
And pulled the night upon. 'Twas day with me—
Perpetual dawn with me.

MILDRED
Come what, come will,
You have been happy: take my hand!

MERTOUN [after a pause]
How good
Your brother is! I figured him a cold—
Shall I say, haughty man?

MILDRED
They told me all.
I know all.

MERTOUN
It will soon be over.

MILDRED
Over?
Oh, what is over? what must I live through
And say, "'tis over"? Is our meeting over?
Have I received in presence of them all
The partner of my guilty love—with brow
Trying to seem a maiden's brow—with lips
Which make believe that when they strive to form
Replies to you and tremble as they strive,
It is the nearest ever they approached
A stranger's... Henry, yours that stranger's... lip—
With cheek that looks a virgin's, and that is...
Ah God, some prodigy of thine will stop
This planned piece of deliberate wickedness
In its birth even! some fierce leprous spot
Will mar the brow's dissimulating! I
Shall murmur no smooth speeches got by heart,
But, frenzied, pour forth all our woeful story,
The love, the shame, and the despair—with them
Round me aghast as round some cursed fount
That should spirt water, and spouts blood. I'll not
...Henry, you do not wish that I should draw
This vengeance down? I'll not affect a grace
That's gone from me—gone once, and gone for ever!

MERTOUN
Mildred, my honour is your own. I'll share
Disgrace I cannot suffer by myself.

A word informs your brother I retract
This morning's offer; time will yet bring forth
Some better way of saving both of us.

MILDRED
I'll meet their faces, Henry!

MERTOUN
When? to-morrow!
Get done with it!

MILDRED
Oh, Henry, not to-morrow!
Next day! I never shall prepare my words
And looks and gestures sooner.—How you must
Despise me!

MERTOUN
Mildred, break it if you choose,
A heart the love of you uplifted—still
Uplifts, thro' this protracted agony,
To heaven! but Mildred, answer me,—first pace
The chamber with me—once again—now, say
Calmly the part, the... what it is of me
You see contempt (for you did say contempt)
—Contempt for you in! I would pluck it off
And cast it from me!—but no—no, you'll not
Repeat that?—will you, Mildred, repeat that?

MILDRED
Dear Henry!

MERTOUN
I was scarce a boy—e'en now
What am I more? And you were infantine
When first I met you; why, your hair fell loose
On either side! My fool's-cheek reddens now
Only in the recalling how it burned
That morn to see the shape of many a dream
—You know we boys are prodigal of charms
To her we dream of—I had heard of one,
Had dreamed of her, and I was close to her,
Might speak to her, might live and die her own,
Who knew? I spoke. Oh, Mildred, feel you not
That now, while I remember every glance
Of yours, each word of yours, with power to test
And weigh them in the diamond scales of pride,
Resolved the treasure of a first and last

Heart's love shall have been bartered at its worth,
—That now I think upon your purity
And utter ignorance of guilt—your own
Or other's guilt—the girlish undisguised
Delight at a strange novel prize—(I talk
A silly language, but interpret, you!)
If I, with fancy at its full, and reason
Scarce in its germ, enjoined you secrecy,
If you had pity on my passion, pity
On my protested sickness of the soul
To sit beside you, hear you breathe, and watch
Your eyelids and the eyes beneath—if you
Accorded gifts and knew not they were gifts—
If I grew mad at last with enterprise
And must behold my beauty in her bower
Or perish—(I was ignorant of even
My own desires—what then were you?) if sorrow—
Sin—if the end came—must I now renounce
My reason, blind myself to light, say truth
Is false and lie to God and my own soul?
Contempt were all of this!

MILDRED
Do you believe...
Or, Henry, I'll not wrong you—you believe
That I was ignorant. I scarce grieve o'er
The past. We'll love on; you will love me still.

MERTOUN
Oh, to love less what one has injured! Dove,
Whose pinion I have rashly hurt, my breast—
Shall my heart's warmth not nurse thee into strength?
Flower I have crushed, shall I not care for thee?
Bloom o'er my crest, my fight-mark and device!
Mildred, I love you and you love me.

MILDRED
Go!
Be that your last word. I shall sleep to-night.

MERTOUN
This is not our last meeting?

MILDRED
One night more.

MERTOUN
And then—think, then!

MILDRED
Then, no sweet courtship-days,
No dawning consciousness of love for us,
No strange and palpitating births of sense
From words and looks, no innocent fears and hopes,
Reserves and confidences: morning's over!

MERTOUN
How else should love's perfected noontide follow?
All the dawn promised shall the day perform.

MILDRED
So may it be! but—
You are cautious, Love?
Are sure that unobserved you scaled the walls?

MERTOUN
Oh, trust me! Then our final meeting's fixed
To-morrow night?

MILDRED
Farewell! stay, Henry... wherefore?
His foot is on the yew-tree bough; the turf
Receives him: now the moonlight as he runs
Embraces him—but he must go—is gone.
Ah, once again he turns—thanks, thanks, my Love!
He's gone. Oh, I'll believe him every word!
I was so young, I loved him so, I had
No mother, God forgot me, and I fell.
There may be pardon yet: all's doubt beyond!
Surely the bitterness of death is past.

ACT II

SCENE.—The Library

Enter **LORD TRESHAM**, hastily

TRESHAM
This way! In, Gerard, quick!

[As **GERARD** enters, **TRESHAM** secures the door.

Now speak! or, wait—

I'll bid you speak directly.

[Seats himself.

Now repeat
Firmly and circumstantially the tale
You just now told me; it eludes me; either
I did not listen, or the half is gone
Away from me. How long have you lived here?
Here in my house, your father kept our woods
Before you?

GERARD
As his father did, my lord.
I have been eating, sixty years almost,
Your bread.

TRESHAM
Yes, yes. You ever were of all
The servants in my father's house, I know,
The trusted one. You'll speak the truth.

GERARD
I'll speak
God's truth. Night after night...

TRESHAM
Since when?

GERARD
At least
A month—each midnight has some man access
To Lady Mildred's chamber.

TRESHAM
Tush, "access"—
No wide words like "access" to me!

GERARD
He runs
Along the woodside, crosses to the South,
Takes the left tree that ends the avenue...

TRESHAM
The last great yew-tree?

GERARD
You might stand upon

The main boughs like a platform. Then he...

TRESHAM
Quick!

GERARD
Climbs up, and, where they lessen at the top,
—I cannot see distinctly, but he throws,
I think—for this I do not vouch—a line
That reaches to the lady's casement—

TRESHAM
Which
He enters not! Gerard, some wretched fool
Dares pry into my sister's privacy!
When such are young, it seems a precious thing
To have approached,—to merely have approached,
Got sight of the abode of her they set
Their frantic thoughts upon. Ha does not enter?
Gerard?

GERARD
There is a lamp that's full i' the midst.
Under a red square in the painted glass
Of Lady Mildred's...

TRESHAM
Leave that name out! Well?
That lamp?

GERARD
Is moved at midnight higher up
To one pane—a small dark-blue pane; he waits
For that among the boughs: at sight of that,
I see him, plain as I see you, my lord,
Open the lady's casement, enter there...

TRESHAM
And stay?

GERARD
An hour, two hours.

TRESHAM
And this you saw
Once?—twice?—quick!

GERARD

Twenty times.

TRESHAM
And what brings you
Under the yew-trees?

GERARD
The first night I left
My range so far, to track the stranger stag
That broke the pale, I saw the man.

TRESHAM
Yet sent
No cross-bow shaft through the marauder?

GERARD
But
He came, my lord, the first time he was seen,
In a great moonlight, light as any day,
FROM Lady Mildred's chamber.

TRESHAM [after a pause]
You have no cause
—Who could have cause to do my sister wrong?

GERARD
Oh, my lord, only once—let me this once
Speak what is on my mind! Since first I noted
All this, I've groaned as if a fiery net
Plucked me this way and that—fire if I turned
To her, fire if I turned to you, and fire
If down I flung myself and strove to die.
The lady could not have been seven years old
When I was trusted to conduct her safe
Through the deer-herd to stroke the snow-white fawn
I brought to eat bread from her tiny hand
Within a month. She ever had a smile
To greet me with—she... if it could undo
What's done, to lop each limb from off this trunk...
All that is foolish talk, not fit for you—
I mean, I could not speak and bring her hurt
For Heaven's compelling. But when I was fixed
To hold my peace, each morsel of your food
Eaten beneath your roof, my birth-place too,
Choked me. I wish I had grown mad in doubts
What it behoved me do. This morn it seemed
Either I must confess to you or die:
Now it is done, I seem the vilest worm

That crawls, to have betrayed my lady.

TRESHAM
No—
No, Gerard!

GERARD
Let me go!

TRESHAM
A man, you say:
What man? Young? Not a vulgar hind? What dress?

GERARD
A slouched hat and a large dark foreign cloak
Wraps his whole form; even his face is hid;
But I should judge him young: no hind, be sure!

TRESHAM
Why?

GERARD
He is ever armed: his sword projects
Beneath the cloak.

TRESHAM
Gerard,—I will not say
No word, no breath of this!

GERARD
Thank, thanks, my lord!

[Goes.

TRESHAM [Paces the room. After a pause]
Oh, thoughts absurd!—as with some monstrous fact
Which, when ill thoughts beset us, seems to give
Merciful God that made the sun and stars,
The waters and the green delights of earth,
The lie! I apprehend the monstrous fact—
Yet know the maker of all worlds is good,
And yield my reason up, inadequate
To reconcile what yet I do behold—
Blasting my sense! There's cheerful day outside:
This is my library, and this the chair
My father used to sit in carelessly
After his soldier-fashion, while I stood
Between his knees to question him: and here

Gerard our grey retainer,—as he says,
Fed with our food, from sire to son, an age,—
Has told a story—I am to believe!
That Mildred... oh, no, no! both tales are true,
Her pure cheek's story and the forester's!
Would she, or could she, err—much less, confound
All guilts of treachery, of craft, of... Heaven
Keep me within its hand!—I will sit here
Until thought settle and I see my course.
Avert, oh God, only this woe from me!

[As he sinks his head between his arms on the table, **GUENDOLEN'S** voice is heard at the door.

Lord Tresham!

[She knocks.

Is Lord Tresham there?

[**TRESHAM**, hastily turning, pulls down the first book above him and opens it.

TRESHAM
Come in!

[She enters.

Ha, Guendolen!—good morning.

GUENDOLEN
Nothing more?

TRESHAM
What should I say more?

GUENDOLEN
Pleasant question! more?
This more. Did I besiege poor Mildred's brain
Last night till close on morning with "the Earl,"
"The Earl"—whose worth did I asseverate
Till I am very fain to hope that... Thorold,
What is all this? You are not well!

TRESHAM
Who, I?
You laugh at me.

GUENDOLEN
Has what I'm fain to hope,

Arrived then? Does that huge tome show some blot
In the Earl's 'scutcheon come no longer back
Than Arthur's time?

TRESHAM
When left you Mildred's chamber?

GUENDOLEN
Oh, late enough, I told you! The main thing
To ask is, how I left her chamber,—sure,
Content yourself, she'll grant this paragon
Of Earls no such ungracious...

TRESHAM
Send her here!

GUENDOLEN
Thorold?

TRESHAM
I mean—acquaint her, Guendolen,
—But mildly!

GUENDOLEN
Mildly?

TRESHAM
Ah, you guessed aright!
I am not well: there is no hiding it.
But tell her I would see her at her leisure—
That is, at once! here in the library!
The passage in that old Italian book
We hunted for so long is found, say, found—
And if I let it slip again... you see,
That she must come—and instantly!

GUENDOLEN
I'll die
Piecemeal, record that, if there have not gloomed
Some blot i' the 'scutcheon!

TRESHAM
Go! or, Guendolen,
Be you at call,—With Austin, if you choose,—
In the adjoining gallery! There go!

[**GUENDOLEN** goes.

Another lesson to me! You might bid
A child disguise his heart's sore, and conduct
Some sly investigation point by point
With a smooth brow, as well as bid me catch
The inquisitorial cleverness some praise.
If you had told me yesterday, "There's one
You needs must circumvent and practise with,
Entrap by policies, if you would worm
The truth out: and that one is—Mildred!" There,
There—reasoning is thrown away on it!
Prove she's unchaste... why, you may after prove
That she's a poisoner, traitress, what you will!
Where I can comprehend nought, nought's to say,
Or do, or think. Force on me but the first
Abomination,—then outpour all plagues,
And I shall ne'er make count of them.

[Enter **MILDRED**.

MILDRED
What book
Is it I wanted, Thorold? Guendolen
Thought you were pale; you are not pale. That book?
That's Latin surely.

TRESHAM
Mildred, here's a line,
(Don't lean on me: I'll English it for you)
"Love conquers all things." What love conquers them?
What love should you esteem—best love?

MILDRED
True love.

TRESHAM
I mean, and should have said, whose love is best
Of all that love or that profess to love?

MILDRED
The list's so long: there's father's, mother's, husband's...

TRESHAM
Mildred, I do believe a brother's love
For a sole sister must exceed them all.
For see now, only see! there's no alloy
Of earth that creeps into the perfect'st gold
Of other loves—no gratitude to claim;
You never gave her life, not even aught

That keeps life—never tended her, instructed,
Enriched her—so, your love can claim no right
O'er her save pure love's claim: that's what I call
Freedom from earthliness. You'll never hope
To be such friends, for instance, she and you,
As when you hunted cowslips in the woods,
Or played together in the meadow hay.
Oh yes—with age, respect comes, and your worth
Is felt, there's growing sympathy of tastes,
There's ripened friendship, there's confirmed esteem:
—Much head these make against the newcomer!
The startling apparition, the strange youth—
Whom one half-hour's conversing with, or, say,
Mere gazing at, shall change (beyond all change
This Ovid ever sang about) your soul
...Her soul, that is,—the sister's soul! With her
'Twas winter yesterday; now, all is warmth,
The green leaf's springing and the turtle's voice,
"Arise and come away!" Come whither?—far
Enough from the esteem, respect, and all
The brother's somewhat insignificant
Array of rights! All which he knows before,
Has calculated on so long ago!
I think such love, (apart from yours and mine,)
Contented with its little term of life,
Intending to retire betimes, aware
How soon the background must be placed for it,
—I think, am sure, a brother's love exceeds
All the world's love in its unworldliness.

MILDRED
What is this for?

TRESHAM
This, Mildred, is it for!
Or, no, I cannot go to it so soon!
That's one of many points my haste left out—
Each day, each hour throws forth its silk-slight film
Between the being tied to you by birth,
And you, until those slender threads compose
A web that shrouds her daily life of hopes
And fears and fancies, all her life, from yours:
So close you live and yet so far apart!
And must I rend this web, tear up, break down
The sweet and palpitating mystery
That makes her sacred? You—for you I mean,
Shall I speak, shall I not speak?

MILDRED
Speak!

TRESHAM
I will.
Is there a story men could—any man
Could tell of you, you would conceal from me?
I'll never think there's falsehood on that lip.
Say "There is no such story men could tell,"
And I'll believe you, though I disbelieve
The world—the world of better men than I,
And women such as I suppose you. Speak!

[After a pause.

Not speak? Explain then! Clear it up then! Move
Some of the miserable weight away
That presses lower than the grave. Not speak?
Some of the dead weight, Mildred! Ah, if I
Could bring myself to plainly make their charge
Against you! Must I, Mildred? Silent still?

[After a pause.

Is there a gallant that has night by night
Admittance to your chamber?

[After a pause.

Then, his name!
Till now, I only had a thought for you:
But now,—his name!

MILDRED
Thorold, do you devise
Fit expiation for my guilt, if fit
There be! 'Tis nought to say that I'll endure
And bless you,—that my spirit yearns to purge
Her stains off in the fierce renewing fire:
But do not plunge me into other guilt!
Oh, guilt enough! I cannot tell his name.

TRESHAM
Then judge yourself! How should I act? Pronounce!

MILDRED
Oh, Thorold, you must never tempt me thus!
To die here in this chamber by that sword

Would seem like punishment: so should I glide,
Like an arch-cheat, into extremest bliss!
'Twere easily arranged for me: but you—
What would become of you?

TRESHAM
And what will now
Become of me? I'll hide your shame and mine
From every eye; the dead must heave their hearts
Under the marble of our chapel-floor;
They cannot rise and blast you. You may wed
Your paramour above our mother's tomb;
Our mother cannot move from 'neath your foot.
We too will somehow wear this one day out:
But with to-morrow hastens here—the Earl!
The youth without suspicion. Face can come
From Heaven and heart from... whence proceed such hearts?
I have dispatched last night at your command
A missive bidding him present himself
To-morrow—here—thus much is said; the rest
Is understood as if 'twere written down—
"His suit finds favor in your eyes." Now dictate
This morning's letter that shall countermand
Last night's—do dictate that!

MILDRED
But, Thorold—if
I will receive him as I said?

TRESHAM
The Earl?

MILDRED
I will receive him.

TRESHAM [starting up]
Ho there! Guendolen!

[**GUENDOLEN** and **AUSTIN** enter

And, Austin, you are welcome, too! Look there!
The woman there!

AUSTIN and **GUENDOLEN**
How? Mildred?

TRESHAM
Mildred once!

Now the receiver night by night, when sleep
Blesses the inmates of her father's house,
—I say, the soft sly wanton that receives
Her guilt's accomplice 'neath this roof which holds
You, Guendolen, you, Austin, and has held
A thousand Treshams—never one like her!
No lighter of the signal-lamp her quick
Foul breath near quenches in hot eagerness
To mix with breath as foul! no loosener
O' the lattice, practised in the stealthy tread,
The low voice and the noiseless come-and-go!
Not one composer of the bacchant's mien
Into—what you thought Mildred's, in a word!
Know her!

GUENDOLEN
Oh, Mildred, look to me, at least!
Thorold—she's dead, I'd say, but that she stands
Rigid as stone and whiter!

TRESHAM
You have heard...

GUENDOLEN
Too much! You must proceed no further.

MILDRED
Yes—
Proceed! All's truth. Go from me!

TRESHAM
All is truth,
She tells you! Well, you know, or ought to know,
All this I would forgive in her. I'd con
Each precept the harsh world enjoins, I'd take
Our ancestors' stern verdicts one by one,
I'd bind myself before then to exact
The prescribed vengeance—and one word of hers,
The sight of her, the bare least memory
Of Mildred, my one sister, my heart's pride
Above all prides, my all in all so long,
Would scatter every trace of my resolve.
What were it silently to waste away
And see her waste away from this day forth,
Two scathed things with leisure to repent,
And grow acquainted with the grave, and die
Tired out if not at peace, and be forgotten?
It were not so impossible to bear.

But this—that, fresh from last night's pledge renewed
Of love with the successful gallant there,
She calmly bids me help her to entice,
Inveigle an unconscious trusting youth
Who thinks her all that's chaste and good and pure,
—Invites me to betray him... who so fit
As honour's self to cover shame's arch-deed?
—That she'll receive Lord Mertoun—(her own phrase)—
This, who could bear? Why, you have heard of thieves,
Stabbers, the earth's disgrace, who yet have laughed,
"Talk not to me of torture—I'll betray
No comrade I've pledged faith to!"—you have heard
Of wretched women—all but Mildreds—tied
By wild illicit ties to losels vile
You'd tempt them to forsake; and they'll reply
"Gold, friends, repute, I left for him, I find
In him, why should I leave him then, for gold,
Repute or friends?"—and you have felt your heart
Respond to such poor outcasts of the world
As to so many friends; bad as you please,
You've felt they were God's men and women still,
So, not to be disowned by you. But she
That stands there, calmly gives her lover up
As means to wed the Earl that she may hide
Their intercourse the surelier: and, for this,
I curse her to her face before you all.
Shame hunt her from the earth! Then Heaven do right
To both! It hears me now—shall judge her then!

[AS **MILDRED** faints and falls, **TRESHAM** rushes out.

AUSTIN
Stay, Tresham, we'll accompany you!

GUENDOLEN
We?
What, and leave Mildred? We? Why, where's my place
But by her side, and where yours but by mine?
Mildred—one word! Only look at me, then!

AUSTIN
No, Guendolen! I echo Thorold's voice.
She is unworthy to behold...

GUENDOLEN
Us two?
If you spoke on reflection, and if I
Approved your speech—if you (to put the thing

At lowest) you the soldier, bound to make
The king's cause yours and fight for it, and throw
Regard to others of its right or wrong,
—If with a death-white woman you can help,
Let alone sister, let alone a Mildred,
You left her—or if I, her cousin, friend
This morning, playfellow but yesterday,
Who said, or thought at least a thousand times,
"I'd serve you if I could," should now face round
And say, "Ah, that's to only signify
I'd serve you while you're fit to serve yourself:
So long as fifty eyes await the turn
Of yours to forestall its yet half-formed wish,
I'll proffer my assistance you'll not need—
When every tongue is praising you, I'll join
The praisers' chorus—when you're hemmed about
With lives between you and detraction—lives
To be laid down if a rude voice, rash eye,
Rough hand should violate the sacred ring
Their worship throws about you,—then indeed,
Who'll stand up for you stout as I?" If so
We said, and so we did,—not Mildred there
Would be unworthy to behold us both,
But we should be unworthy, both of us.
To be beheld by—by—your meanest dog,
Which, if that sword were broken in your face
Before a crowd, that badge torn off your breast,
And you cast out with hooting and contempt,
—Would push his way thro' all the hooters, gain
Your side, go off with you and all your shame
To the next ditch you choose to die in! Austin,
Do you love me? Here's Austin, Mildred,—here's
Your brother says he does not believe half—
No, nor half that—of all he heard! He says,
Look up and take his hand!

AUSTIN
Look up and take
My hand, dear Mildred!

MILDRED
I—I was so young!
Beside, I loved him, Thorold—and I had
No mother; God forgot me: so, I fell.

GUENDOLEN
Mildred!

MILDRED

Require no further! Did I dream
That I could palliate what is done? All's true.
Now, punish me! A woman takes my hand?
Let go my hand! You do not know, I see.
I thought that Thorold told you.

GUENDOLEN

What is this?
Where start you to?

MILDRED

Oh, Austin, loosen me!
You heard the whole of it—your eyes were worse,
In their surprise, than Thorold's! Oh, unless
You stay to execute his sentence, loose
My hand! Has Thorold gone, and are you here?

GUENDOLEN

Here, Mildred, we two friends of yours will wait
Your bidding; be you silent, sleep or muse!
Only, when you shall want your bidding done,
How can we do it if we are not by?
Here's Austin waiting patiently your will!
One spirit to command, and one to love
And to believe in it and do its best,
Poor as that is, to help it—why, the world
Has been won many a time, its length and breadth,
By just such a beginning!

MILDRED

I believe
If once I threw my arms about your neck
And sunk my head upon your breast, that I
Should weep again.

GUENDOLEN

Let go her hand now, Austin!
Wait for me. Pace the gallery and think
On the world's seemings and realities,
Until I call you.

[**AUSTIN** goes.

MILDRED

No—I cannot weep.
No more tears from this brain—no sleep—no tears!
O Guendolen, I love you!

GUENDOLEN
Yes: and "love"
Is a short word that says so very much!
It says that you confide in me.

MILDRED
Confide!

GUENDOLEN
Your lover's name, then! I've so much to learn,
Ere I can work in your behalf!

MILDRED
My friend,
You know I cannot tell his name.

GUENDOLEN
At least
He is your lover? and you love him too?

MILDRED
Ah, do you ask me that,—but I am fallen
So low!

GUENDOLEN
You love him still, then?

MILDRED
My sole prop
Against the guilt that crushes me! I say,
Each night ere I lie down, "I was so young—
I had no mother, and I loved him so!"
And then God seems indulgent, and I dare
Trust him my soul in sleep.

GUENDOLEN
How could you let us
E'en talk to you about Lord Mertoun then?

MILDRED
There is a cloud around me.

GUENDOLEN
But you said
You would receive his suit in spite of this?

MILDRED

I say there is a cloud...

GUENDOLEN
No cloud to me!
Lord Mertoun and your lover are the same!

MILDRED
What maddest fancy...

GUENDOLEN [calling aloud]
Austin! (spare your pains—
When I have got a truth, that truth I keep)—

MILDRED
By all you love, sweet Guendolen, forbear!
Have I confided in you...

GUENDOLEN
Just for this!
Austin!—Oh, not to guess it at the first!
But I did guess it—that is, I divined,
Felt by an instinct how it was: why else
Should I pronounce you free from all that heap
Of sins which had been irredeemable?
I felt they were not yours—what other way
Than this, not yours? The secret's wholly mine!

MILDRED
If you would see me die before his face...

GUENDOLEN
I'd hold my peace! And if the Earl returns
To-night?

MILDRED
 Ah Heaven, he's lost!

GUENDOLEN
 I thought so. Austin!

[Enter **AUSTIN**.

Oh, where have you been hiding?

AUSTIN
Thorold's gone,
I know not how, across the meadow-land.
I watched him till I lost him in the skirts

O' the beech-wood.

GUENDOLEN
Gone? All thwarts us.

MILDRED
Thorold too?

GUENDOLEN
I have thought. First lead this Mildred to her room.
Go on the other side; and then we'll seek
Your brother: and I'll tell you, by the way,
The greatest comfort in the world. You said
There was a clue to all. Remember, Sweet,
He said there was a clue! I hold it. Come!

ACT III

SCENE I.—The End of the Yew-tree Avenue Under Mildred's Window

A light seen through a central red pane

Enter **TRESHAM** through the trees

Again here! But I cannot lose myself.
The heath—the orchard—I have traversed glades
And dells and bosky paths which used to lead
Into green wild-wood depths, bewildering
My boy's adventurous step. And now they tend
Hither or soon or late; the blackest shade
Breaks up, the thronged trunks of the trees ope wide,
And the dim turret I have fled from, fronts
Again my step; the very river put
Its arm about me and conducted me
To this detested spot. Why then, I'll shun
Their will no longer: do your will with me!
Oh, bitter! To have reared a towering scheme
Of happiness, and to behold it razed,
Were nothing: all men hope, and see their hopes
Frustrate, and grieve awhile, and hope anew.
But I... to hope that from a line like ours
No horrid prodigy like this would spring,
Were just as though I hoped that from these old
Confederates against the sovereign day,
Children of older and yet older sires,
Whose living coral berries dropped, as now

On me, on many a baron's surcoat once,
On many a beauty's whimple—would proceed
No poison-tree, to thrust, from hell its root,
Hither and thither its strange snaky arms.
Why came I here? What must I do?

[A bell strikes.

A bell?
Midnight! and 'tis at midnight... Ah, I catch
—Woods, river, plains, I catch your meaning now,
And I obey you! Hist! This tree will serve.

[He retires behind one of the trees. After a pause, enter **MERTOUN** cloaked as before.

MERTOUN
Not time! Beat out thy last voluptuous beat
Of hope and fear, my heart! I thought the clock
I' the chapel struck as I was pushing through
The ferns. And so I shall no more see rise
My love-star! Oh, no matter for the past!
So much the more delicious task to watch
Mildred revive: to pluck out, thorn by thorn,
All traces of the rough forbidden path
My rash love lured her to! Each day must see
Some fear of hers effaced, some hope renewed:
Then there will be surprises, unforeseen
Delights in store. I'll not regret the past.

[The light is placed above in the purple pane.

And see, my signal rises, Mildred's star!
I never saw it lovelier than now
It rises for the last time. If it sets,
'Tis that the re-assuring sun may dawn.

[As he prepares to ascend the last tree of the avenue, **TRESHAM** arrests his arm.

Unhand me—peasant, by your grasp! Here's gold.
'Twas a mad freak of mine. I said I'd pluck
A branch from the white-blossomed shrub beneath
The casement there. Take this, and hold your peace.

TRESHAM
Into the moonlight yonder, come with me!
Out of the shadow!

MERTOUN

I am armed, fool!

TRESHAM
Yes,
Or no? You'll come into the light, or no?
My hand is on your throat—refuse!—

MERTOUN
That voice!
Where have I heard... no—that was mild and slow.
I'll come with you.

[They advance.

TRESHAM
You're armed: that's well. Declare
Your name: who are you?

MERTOUN
Tresham!—she is lost!

TRESHAM
Oh, silent? Do you know, you bear yourself
Exactly as, in curious dreams I've had
How felons, this wild earth is full of, look
When they're detected, still your kind has looked!
The bravo holds an assured countenance,
The thief is voluble and plausible,
But silently the slave of lust has crouched
When I have fancied it before a man.
Your name!

MERTOUN
I do conjure Lord Tresham—ay,
Kissing his foot, if so I might prevail—
That he for his own sake forbear to ask
My name! As heaven's above, his future weal
Or woe depends upon my silence! Vain!
I read your white inexorable face.
Know me, Lord Tresham!

[He throws off his disguises.

TRESHAM
Mertoun!

[After a pause.

Draw now!

MERTOUN
Hear me
But speak first!

TRESHAM
Not one least word on your life!
Be sure that I will strangle in your throat
The least word that informs me how you live
And yet seem what you seem! No doubt 'twas you
Taught Mildred still to keep that face and sin.
We should join hands in frantic sympathy
If you once taught me the unteachable,
Explained how you can live so and so lie.
With God's help I retain, despite my sense,
The old belief—a life like yours is still
Impossible. Now draw!

MERTOUN
Not for my sake,
Do I entreat a hearing—for your sake,
And most, for her sake!

TRESHAM
Ha, ha, what should I
Know of your ways? A miscreant like yourself,
How must one rouse his ire? A blow?—that's pride
No doubt, to him! One spurns him, does one not?
Or sets the foot upon his mouth, or spits
Into his face! Come! Which, or all of these?

MERTOUN
'Twixt him and me and Mildred, Heaven be judge!
Can I avoid this? Have your will, my lord!

[He draws and, after a few passes, falls.

TRESHAM
You are not hurt?

MERTOUN
You'll hear me now!

TRESHAM
But rise!

MERTOUN

Ah, Tresham, say I not "you'll hear me now!"
And what procures a man the right to speak
In his defence before his fellow man,
But—I suppose—the thought that presently
He may have leave to speak before his God
His whole defence?

TRESHAM
Not hurt? It cannot be!
You made no effort to resist me. Where
Did my sword reach you? Why not have returned
My thrusts? Hurt where?

MERTOUN
My lord—

TRESHAM
How young he is!

MERTOUN
Lord Tresham, I am very young, and yet
I have entangled other lives with mine.
Do let me speak, and do believe my speech!
That when I die before you presently,—

TRESHAM
Can you stay here till I return with help?

MERTOUN
Oh, stay by me! When I was less than boy
I did you grievous wrong and knew it not—
Upon my honour, knew it not! Once known,
I could not find what seemed a better way
To right you than I took: my life—you feel
How less than nothing were the giving you
The life you've taken! But I thought my way
The better—only for your sake and hers:
And as you have decided otherwise,
Would I had an infinity of lives
To offer you! Now say—instruct me—think!
Can you, from the brief minutes I have left,
Eke out my reparation? Oh think—think!
For I must wring a partial—dare I say,
Forgiveness from you, ere I die?

TRESHAM
I do
Forgive you.

MERTOUN

Wait and ponder that great word!
Because, if you forgive me, I shall hope
To speak to you of—Mildred!

TRESHAM

Mertoun, haste
And anger have undone us. 'Tis not you
Should tell me for a novelty you're young,
Thoughtless, unable to recall the past.
Be but your pardon ample as my own!

MERTOUN

Ah, Tresham, that a sword-stroke and a drop
Of blood or two, should bring all this about
Why, 'twas my very fear of you, my love
Of you—(what passion like a boy's for one
Like you?)—that ruined me! I dreamed of you—
You, all accomplished, courted everywhere,
The scholar and the gentleman. I burned
To knit myself to you: but I was young,
And your surpassing reputation kept me
So far aloof! Oh, wherefore all that love?
With less of love, my glorious yesterday
Of praise and gentlest words and kindest looks,
Had taken place perchance six months ago.
Even now, how happy we had been! And yet
I know the thought of this escaped you, Tresham!
Let me look up into your face; I feel
'Tis changed above me: yet my eyes are glazed.
Where? where?

[As he endeavours to raise himself, his eye catches the lamp.

Ah, Mildred! What will Mildred do?
Tresham, her life is bound up in the life
That's bleeding fast away! I'll live—must live,
There, if you'll only turn me I shall live
And save her! Tresham—oh, had you but heard!
Had you but heard! What right was yours to set
The thoughtless foot upon her life and mine,
And then say, as we perish, "Had I thought,
All had gone otherwise"? We've sinned and die:
Never you sin, Lord Tresham! for you'll die,
And God will judge you.

TRESHAM

Yes, be satisfied!
That process is begun.

MERTOUN
And she sits there
Waiting for me! Now, say you this to her—
You, not another—say, I saw him die
As he breathed this, "I love her"—you don't know
What those three small words mean! Say, loving her
Lowers me down the bloody slope to death
With memories... I speak to her, not you,
Who had no pity, will have no remorse,
Perchance intend her... Die along with me,
Dear Mildred! 'tis so easy, and you'll 'scape
So much unkindness! Can I lie at rest,
With rude speech spoken to you, ruder deeds
Done to you?—heartless men shall have my heart,
And I tied down with grave-clothes and the worm,
Aware, perhaps, of every blow—oh God!—
Upon those lips—yet of no power to tear
The felon stripe by stripe! Die, Mildred! Leave
Their honourable world to them! For God
We're good enough, though the world casts us out.

[A whistle is heard.

TRESHAM
Ho, Gerard!

[Enter **GERARD**, **AUSTIN** and **GUENDOLEN**, with lights

No one speak! You see what's done.
I cannot bear another voice.

MERTOUN
There's light—
Light all about me, and I move to it.
Tresham, did I not tell you—did you not
Just promise to deliver words of mine
To Mildred?

TRESHAM
I will bear those words to her.

MERTOUN
Now?

TRESHAM

Now. Lift you the body, and leave me
The head.

[As they have half raised **MERTOUN**, he turns suddenly.

MERTOUN
I knew they turned me: turn me not from her!
There! stay you! there!

[Dies.

GUENDOLEN [after a pause]
Austin, remain you here
With Thorold until Gerard comes with help:
Then lead him to his chamber. I must go
To Mildred.

TRESHAM
Guendolen, I hear each word
You utter. Did you hear him bid me give
His message? Did you hear my promise? I,
And only I, see Mildred.

GUENDOLEN
She will die.

TRESHAM
Oh no, she will not die! I dare not hope
She'll die. What ground have you to think she'll die?
Why, Austin's with you!

AUSTIN
Had we but arrived
Before you fought!

TRESHAM
There was no fight at all.
He let me slaughter him—the boy! I'll trust
The body there to you and Gerard—thus!
Now bear him on before me.

AUSTIN
Whither bear him?

TRESHAM
Oh, to my chamber! When we meet there next,
We shall be friends.

[They bear out the body of **MERTOUN**.

Will she die, Guendolen?

GUENDOLEN
Where are you taking me?

TRESHAM
He fell just here.
Now answer me. Shall you in your whole life
—You who have nought to do with Mertoun's fate,
Now you have seen his breast upon the turf,
Shall you e'er walk this way if you can help?
When you and Austin wander arm-in-arm
Through our ancestral grounds, will not a shade
Be ever on the meadow and the waste—
Another kind of shade than when the night
Shuts the woodside with all its whispers up?
But will you ever so forget his breast
As carelessly to cross this bloody turf
Under the black yew avenue? That's well!
You turn your head: and I then?—

GUENDOLEN
What is done
Is done. My care is for the living. Thorold,
Bear up against this burden: more remains
To set the neck to!

TRESHAM
Dear and ancient trees
My fathers planted, and I loved so well!
What have I done that, like some fabled crime
Of yore, lets loose a Fury leading thus
Her miserable dance amidst you all?
Oh, never more for me shall winds intone
With all your tops a vast antiphony,
Demanding and responding in God's praise!
Hers ye are now, not mine! Farewell—farewell!

SCENE II.—Mildred's Chamber

MILDRED alone

He comes not! I have heard of those who seemed
Resourceless in prosperity,—you thought

Sorrow might slay them when she listed; yet
Did they so gather up their diffused strength
At her first menace, that they bade her strike,
And stood and laughed her subtlest skill to scorn.
Oh, 'tis not so with me! The first woe fell,
And the rest fall upon it, not on me:
Else should I bear that Henry comes not?—fails
Just this first night out of so many nights?
Loving is done with. Were he sitting now,
As so few hours since, on that seat, we'd love
No more—contrive no thousand happy ways
To hide love from the loveless, any more.
I think I might have urged some little point
In my defence, to Thorold; he was breathless
For the least hint of a defence: but no,
The first shame over, all that would might fall.
No Henry! Yet I merely sit and think
The morn's deed o'er and o'er. I must have crept
Out of myself. A Mildred that has lost
Her lover—oh, I dare not look upon
Such woe! I crouch away from it! 'Tis she,
Mildred, will break her heart, not I! The world
Forsakes me: only Henry's left me—left?
When I have lost him, for he does not come,
And I sit stupidly... Oh Heaven, break up
This worse than anguish, this mad apathy,
By any means or any messenger!

TRESHAM [without]
Mildred!

MILDRED
Come in! Heaven hears me!

[Enter **TRESHAM**.

You? alone?
Oh, no more cursing!

TRESHAM
Mildred, I must sit.
There—you sit!

MILDRED
Say it, Thorold—do not look
The curse! deliver all you come to say!
What must become of me? Oh, speak that thought
Which makes your brow and cheeks so pale!

TRESHAM
My thought?

MILDRED
All of it!

TRESHAM
How we waded years—ago—
After those water-lilies, till the plash,
I know not how, surprised us; and you dared
Neither advance nor turn back: so, we stood
Laughing and crying until Gerard came—
Once safe upon the turf, the loudest too,
For once more reaching the relinquished prize!
How idle thoughts are, some men's, dying men's!
Mildred,—

MILDRED
You call me kindlier by my name
Than even yesterday: what is in that?

TRESHAM
It weighs so much upon my mind that I
This morning took an office not my own!
I might... of course, I must be glad or grieved,
Content or not, at every little thing
That touches you. I may with a wrung heart
Even reprove you, Mildred; I did more:
Will you forgive me?

MILDRED
Thorold? do you mock?
Oh no... and yet you bid me... say that word!

TRESHAM
Forgive me, Mildred!—are you silent, Sweet?

MILDRED [starting up]
Why does not Henry Mertoun come to-night?
Are you, too, silent?

[Dashing his mantle aside, and pointing to his scabbard, which is empty.

Ah, this speaks for you!
You've murdered Henry Mertoun! Now proceed!
What is it I must pardon? This and all?
Well, I do pardon you—I think I do.

Thorold, how very wretched you must be!

TRESHAM
He bade me tell you...

MILDRED
What I do forbid
Your utterance of! So much that you may tell
And will not—how you murdered him... but, no!
You'll tell me that he loved me, never more
Than bleeding out his life there: must I say
"Indeed," to that? Enough! I pardon you.

TRESHAM
You cannot, Mildred! for the harsh words, yes:
Of this last deed Another's judge: whose doom
I wait in doubt, despondency and fear.

MILDRED
Oh, true! There's nought for me to pardon! True!
You loose my soul of all its cares at once.
Death makes me sure of him for ever! You
Tell me his last words? He shall tell me them,
And take my answer—not in words, but reading
Himself the heart I had to read him late,
Which death...

TRESHAM
Death? You are dying too? Well said
Of Guendolen! I dared not hope you'd die:
But she was sure of it.

MILDRED
Tell Guendolen
I loved her, and tell Austin...

TRESHAM
Him you loved:
And me?

MILDRED
Ah, Thorold! Was't not rashly done
To quench that blood, on fire with youth and hope
And love of me—whom you loved too, and yet
Suffered to sit here waiting his approach
While you were slaying him? Oh, doubtlessly
You let him speak his poor confused boy's-speech
—Do his poor utmost to disarm your wrath

And respite me!—you let him try to give
The story of our love and ignorance,
And the brief madness and the long despair—
You let him plead all this, because your code
Of honour bids you hear before you strike:
But at the end, as he looked up for life
Into your eyes—you struck him down!

TRESHAM
No! No!
Had I but heard him—had I let him speak
Half the truth—less—had I looked long on him
I had desisted! Why, as he lay there,
The moon on his flushed cheek, I gathered all
The story ere he told it: I saw through
The troubled surface of his crime and yours
A depth of purity immovable,
Had I but glanced, where all seemed turbidest
Had gleamed some inlet to the calm beneath;
I would not glance: my punishment's at hand.
There, Mildred, is the truth! and you—say on—
You curse me?

MILDRED
As I dare approach that Heaven
Which has not bade a living thing despair,
Which needs no code to keep its grace from stain,
But bids the vilest worm that turns on it
Desist and be forgiven,—I—forgive not,
But bless you, Thorold, from my soul of souls!

[Falls on his neck.

There! Do not think too much upon the past!
The cloud that's broke was all the same a cloud
While it stood up between my friend and you;
You hurt him 'neath its shadow: but is that
So past retrieve? I have his heart, you know;
I may dispose of it: I give it you!
It loves you as mine loves! Confirm me, Henry!

[Dies.

TRESHAM
I wish thee joy, Beloved! I am glad
In thy full gladness!

GUENDOLEN [without]

Mildred! Tresham!

[Entering with **AUSTIN**.

Thorold,
I could desist no longer. Ah, she swoons!
That's well.

TRESHAM
Oh, better far than that!

GUENDOLEN
She's dead!
Let me unlock her arms!

TRESHAM
She threw them thus
About my neck, and blessed me, and then died:
You'll let them stay now, Guendolen!

AUSTIN
Leave her
And look to him! What ails you, Thorold?

GUENDOLEN
White
As she, and whiter! Austin! quick—this side!

AUSTIN
A froth is oozing through his clenched teeth;
Both lips, where they're not bitten through, are black:
Speak, dearest Thorold!

TRESHAM
Something does weigh down
My neck beside her weight: thanks: I should fall
But for you, Austin, I believe!—there, there,
'Twill pass away soon!—ah,—I had forgotten:
I am dying.

GUENDOLEN
Thorold—Thorold—why was this?

TRESHAM
I said, just as I drank the poison off,
The earth would be no longer earth to me,
The life out of all life was gone from me.
There are blind ways provided, the fore-done

Heart-weary player in this pageant-world
Drops out by, letting the main masque defile
By the conspicuous portal: I am through—
Just through!

GUENDOLEN
Don't leave him, Austin! Death is close.

TRESHAM
Already Mildred's face is peacefuller,
I see you, Austin—feel you; here's my hand,
Put yours in it—you, Guendolen, yours too!
You're lord and lady now—you're Treshams; name
And fame are yours: you hold our 'scutcheon up.
Austin, no blot on it! You see how blood
Must wash one blot away: the first blot came
And the first blood came. To the vain world's eye
All's gules again: no care to the vain world,
From whence the red was drawn!

AUSTIN
No blot shall come!

TRESHAM
I said that: yet it did come. Should it come,
Vengeance is God's, not man's. Remember me!

[Dies.

GUENDOLEN [letting fall the pulseless arm]
Ah, Thorold, we can but—remember you!

Robert Browning – A Short Biography

He is the equal of any Victorian Poet that could be mentioned. However, Browning continues to be in the shadow of Tennyson, Arnold, Hopkins, Morris and many others.

Robert Browning was born on May 7th, 1812 in Walworth in the parish of Camberwell, London. He was baptized on June 14th, 1812, at Lock's Fields Independent Chapel, York Street, Walworth.

Browning's early years were certainly very interesting. His mother was an excellent pianist and a very devout evangelical Christian. His father, who worked as a clerk at the Bank of England, was also an artist, scholar, antiquarian, and collector of books and pictures. Indeed, he amassed more than 6,000 volumes of rare books including works in Greek, Hebrew, Latin, French, Italian, and Spanish. For the young and curious Browning, it was a wonderful resource, added to which his father was a guiding force in his education.

Many accounts attest that Browning was already proficient at reading and writing by the age of five. He is said to have been a bright but anxious student and to have studied and learnt Latin, Greek, and French by the time he was fourteen. From fourteen to sixteen he was educated at home, tutored in music, drawing, dancing, and horsemanship. Certainly, language and the arts were two areas the young Browning both absorbed and pushed himself towards.

At the age of twelve he wrote a volume of Byronic verse he called Incondita, which his parents attempted to have published. The attempts were unsuccessful and, disappointed, Browning destroyed the work.

In 1825, a cousin gave Browning a collection of Percy Bysshe Shelley's poetry; Browning was so enamored with the poems that he asked for the rest of Shelley's works for his thirteenth birthday. In fact, Browning then went the extra mile, declaring himself to be both a vegetarian and an atheist in honour of his hero.

Intriguingly it seems that the rejection of his first volume didn't dim his appreciation of other poets, but it appears to have stopped him writing any poems between the ages of thirteen and twenty.

In 1828, Browning enrolled at the newly-opened University of London. He was uncomfortable with the experience and he soon left, anxious to read and absorb at his own pace.

His education which, overall is notably rambling and lacks a structure that many of his artistic contemporaries enjoyed, i.e. excellent public schooling and then a degree at Oxford or Cambridge, may present many of his critics with ammunition to criticize, but alternatively his hap-hazard education certainly contributed to many of the references that baffled both critics and his audience, but they tellingly show the breath and scale of what he could turn words too. What others would call obscure references were, to Browning, remarkably obvious.

Browning's early career was very promising. His long poem Pauline (of which only a fragment was ever finished and published) brought him to the attention of the Pre-Raphaelite master Dante Gabriel Rossetti and his difficult Paracelsus (published in 1835) was warmly admired by both Dickens and Wordsworth.

In the 1830s he met the actor William Macready and was encouraged to develop and turn his talents to the stage by writing verse drama. But these plays, including Strafford, which ran for five nights in 1837, and those contained within the Bells and Pomegranates series, were, for the most part, unsuccessful.

During this period Browning began to discover that his real talents lay in taking a single character and allowing that character to discover more about himself by revealing further personal aspects of himself in his speeches; the dramatic monologue. The techniques he developed through this—especially the use of diction, rhythm, and symbol—are regarded as his most important contribution to poetry. They would later influence such major poets of the 20th Century as Ezra Pound, T. S. Eliot, and Robert Frost.

By 1840, with the publication of Sordello, the tide turned somewhat. Many thought he was being deliberately obscure, opaque beyond measure and his poetry for the next decade or so was not eagerly acquired or talked about.

As Browning attempted to rehabilitate his career he began a relationship with Elizabeth Barrett in 1845. He had read her poems and, being totally charmed by their quality, was determined to meet her. The poetess was better known than the younger Browning but suffered from a debilitating illness and was also subject to the harsh behaviour of her over-bearing father. Nevertheless, the new couple were soon inseparable.

Her father, as he did with any of his children that married, disinherited her. Despite this she had some money from her own resources and sensing that the best outcome for both the relationship and her own health was to move abroad the couple did just that. After a private marriage at St Marylebone Parish Church, in September 1846, they journeyed to Europe to honeymoon in Paris.

Their new life now took them to Italy, first to Pisa and a little later to Florence. There they absorbed life and one another.

But in the short term the literary assault on Browning's work did not let up. He was now criticized by such patrician writers as Charles Kingsley for his abandonment of England for foreign lands. Browning could do little to answer these attacks except to compose with his pen and continue with his poetical journey.

The Browning's were well respected, and even famous. Elizabeth health began to improve, she grew stronger and in 1849, at the age of 43, between four miscarriages, she gave birth to a son, Robert Wiedeman Barrett Browning, whom they nicknamed "Penini" or "Pen",

Intriguingly despite his growing reputation and return to form as a poet he was more often than not known as 'Elizabeth Barrett's husband'.

Work flowed from his pen that was to ensure his reputation as one of England's leading poets. When his collection Men and Women was published in 1855 it contained some of his finest lines. It was dedicated to Elizabeth. Life had begun to smile handsome rewards upon the Brownings.

Victorian society was very much taken with all things spiritualist. It was not enough to have command of much of the globe through Empire, they wished to know and explore wherever they could. The spirit world beckoned their interest. Browning dissented from this view believing it was all a hoax and a fraud. Elizabeth, however, was inclined to believe and this caused several disagreements between the couple.

They attended a séance by Daniel Dunglas Home, in July 1855. (Home was a famous and clamored after Scottish physical medium with the reported ability to levitate and speak with the dead). It is said that during this séance a spirit face materialised. Home then claimed it was the face of Browning's son who had died in infancy. Browning seized the 'materialisation' which turned out to be Home's bare foot. Browning had never lost a son in infancy.

After the séance, Browning wrote an angry letter to The Times, in which he said: "the whole display of hands, spirit utterances etc., was a cheat and imposture."

The Browning's time in Italy were immensely rewarding years for both their personal and professional lives. Browning encouraged her to include Sonnets from the Portuguese in her published works, these beautiful poems are undoubtedly one of the highlights of English love poetry.

Elizabeth had become quite politicised during these years. Engrossed in Italian politics (which was continuing to slowly re-unify the country), she issued a small volume of political poems entitled Poems before Congress (1860) most of which were written to express her sympathy with the Italian cause after the earlier outbreak of The Second Italian Independence War in 1859. In England they caused uproar. Conservative magazines such as Blackwood's and the Saturday Review labelled her a fanatic. She dedicated the book to her husband.

But in 1861 tragedy struck.

The couple had spent the winter of 1860–61 in Rome when Elizabeth's health deteriorated again and they returned to Florence in early June. However, these turned out to be her final weeks. Only morphine would now still the pain. She died in Browning's arms on June 29th, 1861. Browning said that she died "smilingly, happily, and with a face like a girl's .... Her last word was .... "Beautiful".

Her burial took place in the nearby Protestant English Cemetery of Florence. The local people were deeply saddened, and shops closed their doors in grief and respect.

Browning and their son were obviously devastated. Unable to bear being in Florence without Elizabeth they soon returned to London to live at 19 Warwick Crescent, Maida Vale.

As he re-integrated himself back into the London literary scene he began to finally receive the proper praise, respect and reputation that his works deserved.

Browning went on to publish Dramatis Personæ (1864), and The Ring and the Book (1868–1869). The latter, based on an "old yellow book" which told of a seventeenth-century Italian murder trial, received wide and generous critical acclaim. Although by now he was in the twilight of a long and prolific career, that had achieved some notable ups and downs, he was respected and indeed renowned for his talents and works.

In 1878, he revisited Italy for the first time since Elizabeth's death. He would return there on several further occasions but never to Florence.

Such was the esteem he was held in that The Browning Society was founded in 1881. Although he had never obtained a degree (something that set him apart from many other Victorian poets) he was now awarded honorary degrees from Oxford University in 1882 and then the University of Edinburgh in 1884.

In 1887, Browning produced the major work of his later years, Parleyings with Certain People of Importance in Their Day. Browning now spoke with his own voice as he engaged in a series of dialogues with long-forgotten figures of literary, artistic, and philosophic history. Unfortunately, both the critics and public were completely baffled by this.

On April 7th, 1889 Browning attended a dinner party at the home of his friend, the artist Rudolf Lehmann. The highlight of which was a recording made on a wax cylinder on an Edison cylinder phonograph. On the recording, which still exists, Browning recites part of How They Brought the Good News from Ghent to Aix, and can even be heard apologising when he forgets the words.

The recording was first played in 1890 on the anniversary of his death, at a gathering of his admirers, it was said to be the first time anyone's voice 'had been heard from beyond the grave'.

His last work Asolando: Fancies and Facts (1889), returned to his brief and concise lyric verse that was so popular. It was published on the day of his death on December 12th, 1889, Robert Browning was at his son's home Ca' Rezzonico in Venice.

He was buried in Poets' Corner in Westminster Abbey; his grave lies immediately adjacent to that of Alfred Tennyson.

Among the many who have publicly acknowledged their literary debt to him are Henry James, Oscar Wilde, George Bernard Shaw, G. K. Chesterton, Ezra Pound, Jorge Luis Borges, and Vladimir Nabokov.

Robert Browning - A Concise Bibliography

Here follows a list of the plays and poetry volumes published during his lifetime. Poems of particular worth are noted from within those volumes.

Pauline: A Fragment of a Confession (1833)
Paracelsus (1835)
Strafford (play) (1837)
Sordello (1840)
Bells and Pomegranates No. I: Pippa Passes (play) (1841)
  The Year's at the Spring
Bells and Pomegranates No. II: King Victor and King Charles (play) (1842)
Bells and Pomegranates No. III: Dramatic Lyrics (1842)
  Porphyria's Lover
  Soliloquy of the Spanish Cloister
  My Last Duchess
  The Pied Piper of Hamelin
  Count Gismond
  Johannes Agricola in Meditation
Bells and Pomegranates No. IV: The Return of the Druses (play) (1843)
Bells and Pomegranates No. V: A Blot in the 'Scutcheon (play) (1843)
Bells and Pomegranates No. VI: Colombe's Birthday (play) (1844)
Bells and Pomegranates No. VII: Dramatic Romances and Lyrics (1845)
  The Laboratory
  How They Brought the Good News from Ghent to Aix
  The Bishop Orders His Tomb at Saint Praxed's Church
  The Lost Leader
  Home Thoughts from Abroad
  Meeting at Night
Bells and Pomegranates No. VIII: Luria and A Soul's Tragedy (plays) (1846)
Christmas-Eve and Easter-Day (1850)
An Essay on Percy Bysshe Shelley (essay) (1852)
Two Poems (1854)
Men and Women (1855)
  Love Among the Ruins